Chapter 5

Earth and Sky

Weathering and erosion have changed the Grand Canyon.

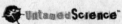

myscienceonLine.com

UntamedScience™
Watch the Ecogeeks learn
about Earth and sky.

Got it? ⏱ **60-Second Video**
Take one minute to learn
about Earth and sky.

Science Songs
Listen to a catchy tune about
Earth and sky.

Explore It! Animation
Quick and easy experiments
about Earth and sky.

Investigate It! Simulation
Find out how rocks can crack
in this online lab.

What does the rock look like?

Earth and Sky

Tell about the land in the picture.

What can you tell about Earth and sky?

Go to www.myscienceonline.com and click on: ✕

UntamedScience
Watch the Ecogeeks in this wild video.

Got it? 60-Second Video
Take one minute to learn science!

Explore It! Animation
Watch your experiment online!

How much water and land are on Earth?

Materials
inflatable globe

☐ **1. Observe** Find water and land on the globe.

☐ **2.** Toss the globe.

☐ **3.** Catch the globe.

☐ **4. Collect Data** Is the tip of your finger on water or land? Put a mark in the chart.

> **Inquiry Skill**
> You **interpret data** when you use your chart to answer a question.

Water	Land

☐ **5.** Repeat the steps 9 more times.

Explain Your Results

6. Interpret Data Use your chart to answer the question. Is there more water or land on Earth? Explain.

Compare and Contrast

You **compare** when you tell
how things are alike.
You **contrast** when you tell
how things are different.

Appalachian Mountains

Mountains

Mountains are very high.
The Rocky Mountains are rough.
The Appalachian Mountains
are not.
The Rocky Mountains are higher
than the Appalachian Mountains.

Rocky Mountains

Practice It!

Write how the mountains are alike and different.

Compare	Contrast
The mountains are high.	The rocky mountains is higher.

What is on Earth?

Envision It!

lake

Draw another kind of land or water.

My Planet Diary

Connections

Read Together

Long ago people known as the Incas lived in the mountains in South America. It was hard to grow crops in the mountains. The Incas built flat pieces of land called terraces so they could grow crops. Today some people do not have land to grow crops and other plants. They use pots and planters.

Write how you might grow plants where you live.

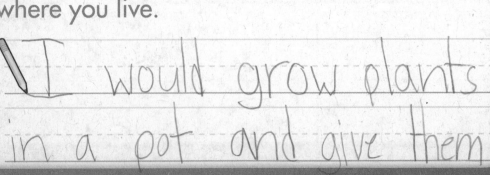

I would grow plants in a pot and give them water.

UNLOCK THE BIG ?

I will know that land, water, and living things are found on Earth.

Word to Know

soil

Land, Water, and Air

Earth is made of many things.

Earth has land.

Earth has water.

The surface of Earth has more water than land.

Earth has air all around it.

Color the land green.
Color the water blue.

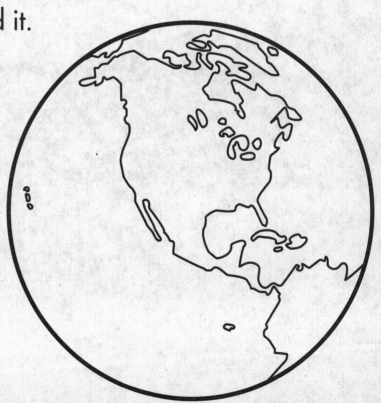

Kinds of Land

Earth has many different kinds of land.
Plains are large, flat areas of land.
Hills are where the land gets higher.
Mountains are the highest kind of land.
An island is land with water all
around it.

Label the plains,
mountains, and island.

Plains

Island

Mountains

The Blue Ridge Mountains
rise above the land
around them.

Rocks and Soil

Earth's land has rocks and soil.

Rocks are hard.

Rocks can be many colors.

Soil is the top layer of Earth.

Soil can be soft.

Underline two things that are found on Earth.

rocks and soil

⊙ **Compare and Contrast Write** one way rocks and soil are different.

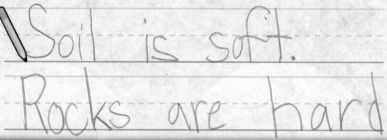

Soil is soft.
Rocks are hard

At-Home Lab

Kinds of Landforms
Draw one kind of land near where you live. Draw another kind of land. Write how they are the same. Write how they are different.

Water on Earth

Earth has many places with water.

A river is water that flows across land.

Lakes have land all around them.

The ocean is a large area of salt water.

The ocean covers most of Earth.

Match the word to the picture.
Draw a line.

river   lake   ocean

Living Things

Living things are on land.
Living things are in soil.
Living things are in water.

Circle living things on land.
Draw an X on living things in water.

167

Lesson 2

What are rocks and soil?

Tell how you can group the rocks.

Inquiry **Explore It!**

What are soils like?

☐ **1.** Put a spoonful of each soil on a paper plate.

☐ **2. Observe.** Draw. Show colors. Tell how each soil feels.

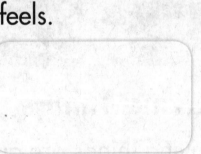

Loam   Sandy Soil

Materials

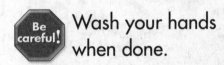

paper plate   loam and sandy soil (whole class use)

hand lens   spoons

Be careful! Wash your hands when done.

Explain Your Results

3. Communicate Describe what you see in the soil.

_____

- - - - - - - - - - - - - - - - - -

_____

UNLOCK
THE BIG
?
I will know how to describe rocks and soil.

Word to Know

humus

Rocks

Rocks are nonliving things.
Rocks come from Earth.

Rocks can be different sizes.
Rocks can be different shapes.
Rocks can be different colors.
Rocks can feel smooth or rough.

Write about the rock in the picture.

There is krystals in the rock.

Crystals formed inside this rock.

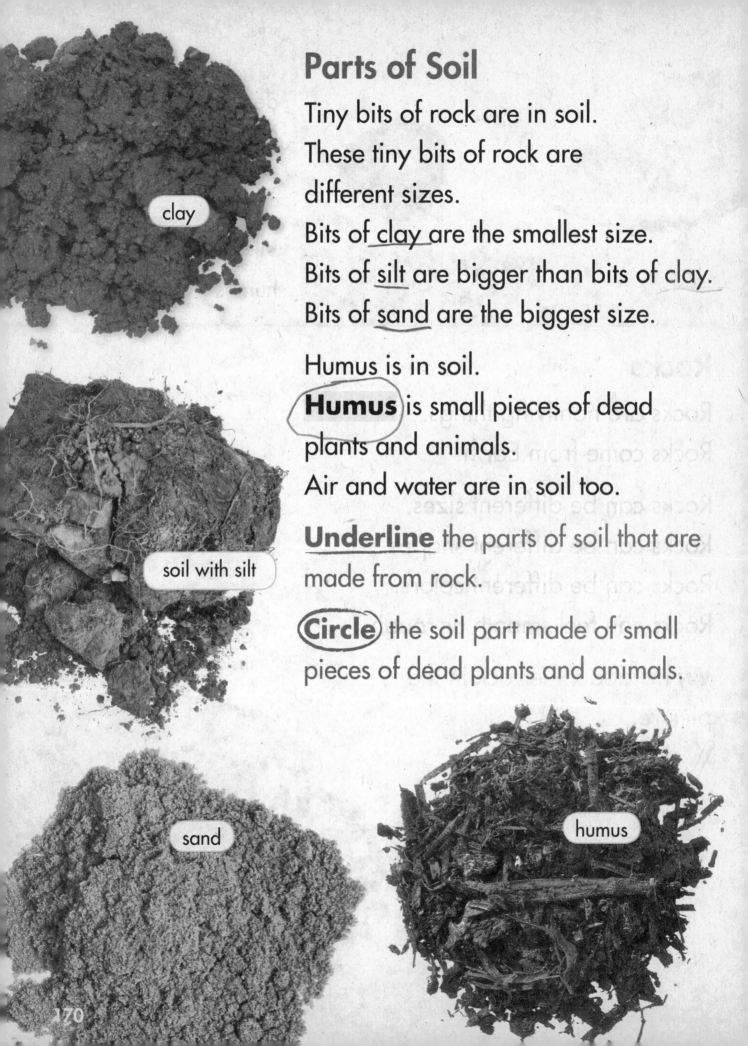

Parts of Soil

Tiny bits of rock are in soil.
These tiny bits of rock are
different sizes.
Bits of <u>clay</u> are the smallest size.
Bits of <u>silt</u> are bigger than bits of clay.
Bits of <u>sand</u> are the biggest size.

Humus is in soil.
Humus is small pieces of dead
plants and animals.
Air and water are in soil too.

Underline the parts of soil that are
made from rock.

Circle the soil part made of small
pieces of dead plants and animals.

clay

soil with silt

sand

humus

Clay Soil

Soils from different places can have different parts.

Soils can be different colors.

Soils can be smooth or rough.

Clay soil is made mostly of clay.

Clay soil can feel smooth and sticky.

Some clay soil is red.

Clay soil does not have a lot of air.

Many plants do not grow well in clay soil.

Write about the soil in the picture.

It do not have a lot of air.

This soil is made of clay.

Soil With Silt and Sandy Soil

Some soil is mostly made of silt.
Soil with silt can feel smooth.
Soil with silt is often brown.
Plants often grow well in soil with silt.

Sandy soil is mostly made of sand.
Sandy soil feels dry and rough.
Often sandy soil is tan.
Sandy soil does not hold water well.
Most plants do not grow well in sandy soil.

These hills have soil with silt.

⦿ Compare and Contrast
Write one way that soil with silt is different from sandy soil.

_____

- - - - - - - - - - - - - - - - - -

This desert has sandy soil.

Loam soil is best for gardens.

loam

Loam

Loam has (clay), (silt), and (sand).

Loam has (humus) too.

Loam feels wet.

Loam is often dark brown.

Loam has the right amount of (water) and (air).

Plants grow well in loam soil.

(Circle) what is in loam.

Draw how you could use loam.

173

Lesson 3

What changes land?

before

This volcano erupted.

Inquiry **Explore It!**

How does Earth's surface move during an earthquake?

Materials

2 sandpaper blocks

☑ 1. Push the blocks together. Slide them past each other.

☑ 2. Push the blocks together hard. Slide them past each other.

Explain Your Results

3. Did the blocks move smoothly both times? Explain.

4. **Infer** An earthquake happens **(fast/slow)**. Tell why.

174

(after)

Tell how the land changed.

Words to Know

weathering
erosion

Changes on Earth

Earth is always changing.
Some changes happen fast.
A truck digs a hole in the ground.
This is a fast change.
Other changes are very slow.
A river flows through land.
This changes land slowly.

Underline a way Earth can change fast.

This truck moves rocks and soil.

The Colorado River makes the Grand Canyon wider and deeper.

Earthquakes and Volcanoes

Earthquakes happen fast.

An earthquake can cause land to crack.

Volcanoes cause fast changes too.

Volcanoes can explode.

Rock and ash from a volcano can cover land.

earthquake

volcano

◉ **Compare and Contrast Write** how
earthquakes and volcanoes are alike.

Weathering and Erosion

Weathering and erosion change land slowly.

Weathering is when water or ice breaks down rocks.

Erosion is when wind or water moves rocks and soil.

Weathering and erosion can take a long time!

weathering

erosion

Circle what causes weathering.
Underline what causes erosion.
Tell one change to land that happens fast and one that happens slowly.

Lightning Lab

Erosion
Pour sand into one end of a pan. Raise that end. Slowly pour water over the sand. Write where the sand goes.

Lesson 4

How do people use natural resources?

Tell why you think people collect cans.

Inquiry **Explore It!**

How does a well work?

People need water. Some people get the water they need from wells.

☐ **1.** Put a tube in a bowl.
Pour gravel around the tube.
The tube is a **model** of a well.

☐ **2.** Make it rain. Pour water on the gravel.
Observe.

Materials

plastic bowl

cardboard tube

plastic cup with water

plastic cup with gravel

Explain Your Result

3. Infer How did the water move in your model?

_____

_____

_____

178

UNLOCK THE BIG ?

I will know how people use natural resources.

Words to Know

natural   reuse
 resource   recycle
reduce

Natural Resources

People use Earth materials for
many things.
A **natural resource** is a useful
material found on Earth.
Water is a natural resource.
Rocks and soil are natural resources.
Plants and animals are natural
resources too.

Circle one natural resource in the picture.
Write how you use the natural resource.

Sunlight and Wood

Sunlight is a natural resource.
People use heat and light from the sun.

Sunlight makes plants grow.

Sunlight cannot be used up.

Wood is a natural resource.
People use wood to build many things.
People burn wood for heat.
People can plant trees to grow
more wood.

Wood is used
to build houses.

Circle the natural resource that cannot be used up.
Underline how people can get more wood.
Write about something else people make with wood.

_____

_____

_____

Oil and Copper

Oil is a natural resource.

Gasoline is made from oil.

People use energy from gasoline
to power cars.

Oil can be used up.

Copper is a natural resource.

People use copper to make wire.

Copper can be used up.

Suppose all the oil on Earth is used up.
Tell what you think might happen.

Gasoline is a source of energy.

Copper is a metal that comes
from Earth.

Reduce, Reuse, and Recycle

You can use natural resources wisely.
You can reduce what you use.
Reduce means to use less.
You can turn off the lights
when you leave a room.

You can reuse things.
Reuse means to use again.
You can wash glass jars
and use them again.

Tell one way you can reduce
how much paper you use.

Draw one way you can
reuse a glass jar.

Go Green

Care for Earth
Write a plan for how
you can care for
Earth. Share your plan
with your family. Do
your plan.

You can recycle.

Recycle means to make used materials into new things.

You can recycle paper, plastic, and glass. You can recycle many other things too.

Write one thing you use that is made from recycled material.

_____

_____

Milk jugs are used to make things like the bench below.

MADE OF RECYCLED MATERIALS

What is the sun?

Envision It!

Circle what the sun warms.

Explore It!

How can the sun make temperatures change?

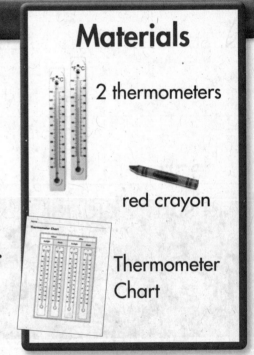

Materials

2 thermometers

red crayon

Thermometer Chart

☐ **1. Observe** the thermometers. Color in the lines on the chart.

☐ **2.** Put one in sunlight. Put one in shade.

☐ **3.** Wait. Observe. Color in the lines.

☐ **4.** Which thermometer warmed up more?

_____

_____

Explain Your Results

5. Infer How did sunlight change the temperature?

_____

_____

The Nearest Star

A star is a big ball of hot gas.
The sun is a star.
The **sun** is the star that
is nearest to Earth.
The sun is bigger
than Earth.
The sun looks small
because it is far away.
You can see the sun
in the day sky.

The sun is very hot
and bright.

⊙ **Cause and Effect**

Circle the words that tell
why the sun looks small.

185

Why We Need the Sun

The sun helps us.

The sun warms the land.

The sun warms the water.

The sun warms the air.

Living things need heat from the sun.

The sun lights Earth.

Plants need light from the sun to grow.

We use light from the sun to see.

Write one reason why living things need the sun.

The sun lights earth.

The sun makes the day sky bright.

Out in the Sun

The sun can harm us too. It is important to be careful in the sun. Too much sun can hurt your skin and eyes. Sunscreen and a hat can protect you from the sun. Some sunglasses can protect your eyes from the sun. You should never look at the sun.

Underline one way the sun harms us.

Circle two things that protect these children from the sun.

Lightning Lab

Heat from the Sun
Get two pieces of clay. Put one piece in sunlight. Put the other in shade. Wait 10 minutes. Write how each feels.

187

What causes day and night?

Envision It!

Tell how day and night are different.

my planet diary INVENTION!

Read Together

Scientists use telescopes to observe the night sky. The first telescope was invented by Hans Lippershey. Hans Lippershey invented the telescope over 400 years ago. Newer telescopes can help you see things in more detail. People have made many discoveries using telescopes.

Write what you would observe with a telescope.

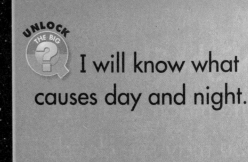

Day Sky

The sun is in the day sky.

The sun makes the day sky bright.

You may see clouds in the day sky.

You may see birds in the day sky.

Sometimes you can see the moon
in the day sky too.

day sky

Write about the day sky
in the picture.

Night Sky

The moon and stars are in the night sky.
You may see clouds in the night sky.
You may see birds in the night sky too.

night sky

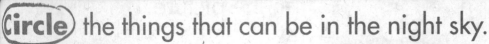

Circle the things that can be in the night sky.

Moon

The moon moves around Earth.
Light from the sun shines on the moon.
You only see the part of the moon lit
by the sun.
The moon looks a little different
each night.
The moon looks the same again
about every 29 days.

Draw the different ways the
moon might look.

At-Home Lab

Changes in the Sky
Observe the sky when the sun rises. Observe the sky when the sun sets. Tell your family about what you see. Never look directly at the sun.

Sunrise and Sunset

The sun seems to rise each day. The sky becomes light. The sun seems to move across the sky during the day. The sun seems to set at night. The sky becomes dark.

Tell how the sky changes from day to night.

Day and Night

The sun looks like it is
moving but it is not.
Earth is moving.
Earth spins around
and around.
One spin around is
called a **rotation.**
Earth makes one rotation every day.

Earth is always spinning.

It is day when your part of Earth
faces toward the sun.
It is night when your part of Earth
faces away from the sun.
The rotation of Earth causes day
and night.

Write what causes day and night.

How can rocks crack?

Follow a Procedure

☐ **1.** Push the foil end of the sponge into the plaster. Keep the other end of the sponge out.

☐ **2.** Wait 1 day. Pull out the sponge. Do not pull out the foil. **Observe. Record.**

☐ **3.** Fill the foil with water. Put the cup in a freezer. Wait 1 day.

☐ **4.** Observe the cup. How has the plaster changed? Record your data.

Materials

plastic cup with plaster of paris

sponge with foil

water

safety goggles

latex-free gloves (optional)

Inquiry Skill

In an **investigation** you observe carefully and record your results.

Be careful!

Wear safety goggles.

Wash your hands if you get plaster on them.

Do not eat plaster or get it in your eyes.

Observations

After 1 day	
After freezing	

Be careful! Wash your hands when you finish.

Analyze and Conclude

5. Draw a Conclusion What caused the changes?

_____

_____

6. UNLOCK THE BIG ? **Infer** How are some cracks made in Earth's rocks?

_____

_____

_____

_____

_____

Science
Technology
Engineering
Math

STEM
Read Together

Aluminum

You can find materials such as aluminum on Earth. Aluminum is a metal. It is not heavy. It is light. It is shiny. Aluminum is found in many different products. It is in foil and some cans. Aluminum is in some cars and trucks too. Engineers use aluminum to build parts of some cars and trucks. Cars and trucks made with aluminum are lighter than other cars and trucks. They use less gas. This helps the environment.

Melted aluminum is poured into molds and can become part of a fire truck or an aluminum can.

Aluminum is a light metal. What other ways might engineers use aluminum?

Vocabulary Smart Cards

soil
humus
weathering
erosion
natural
 resource
reduce
reuse
recycle
sun
rotation

Play a Game!

Cut out the cards.

Work with a group.

Tape a card to the back of each group member.

Have each member guess what his or her word is by giving clues.

erosion

erosión

soil

suelo

natural resource

recurso natural

humus

humus

reduce

reducir

weathering

meteorización

the top layer of Earth

la capa superior de la Tierra

when wind or water moves rocks and soil

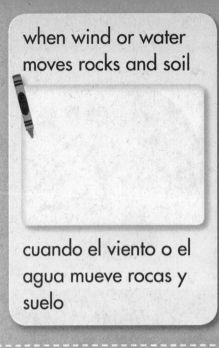

cuando el viento o el agua mueve rocas y suelo

small bits of dead plants and animals in soil

restos de plantas y animales muertos en el suelo

a useful material found in nature

material útil que se encuentra en la naturaleza

when water or ice breaks down rocks

cuando el agua o el hielo rompe las rocas

to use less

usar menos

rotation

rotación

reuse

reutilizar

recycle

reciclar

sun

Sol

to use again

volver a usar

one spin around

dar una vuelta sobre
sí mismo

to make used
materials into new
materials

convertir materiales
usados en materiales
nuevos

a big ball of hot gas

bola muy grande de
gas caliente

REVIEW THE BIG ? What can you tell about Earth and sky?

Lesson 1 What is on Earth?

- Earth has different kinds of land and water.
- Rocks and soil are on Earth's surface.

Lesson 2 What are rocks and soil?

- Rocks can be different colors and shapes.
- Humus is in many kinds of soil.

Lesson 3 What changes land?

- Volcanoes and earthquakes change land.
- Weathering and erosion change land too.

Lesson 4 How do people use natural resources?

- Rocks and soil are natural resources.
- You can reduce, reuse, and recycle.

Lesson 5 What is the sun?

- The sun warms and lights Earth.
- The sun can harm your skin and eyes.

Lesson 6 What causes day and night?

- The sun makes the day sky bright.
- The rotation of Earth causes day and night.

Lesson 1

1. Exemplify Draw two things that are found on Earth.

Lesson 2

2. Apply Write about clay soil.

Lesson 3

⊙ **3. Compare and Contrast Write** how erosion and earthquakes are different.

Lesson 4

4. Vocabulary Draw an ✗ on the natural resource.

Lesson 5

5. Explain Why do we need the sun?

Lesson 6

6. What is NOT seen in the night sky? **Fill in** the bubble.

   Ⓐ birds   Ⓒ clouds

   Ⓑ moon   Ⓓ sun

Got it?

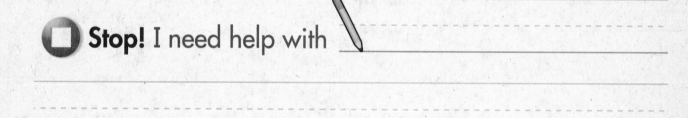

☐ **Stop!** I need help with

▶ **Go!** Now I know

This is your book.

You can write in it.